Mémé's Memory Quilt

Dedication and Acknowledgments from the Author

To Rachel LeDuc – thank you for the gift of your artistry to this book. You've brought my story to life, and for that I will be forever grateful.

To Robin Skarbek – thank you tremendously for your dedication to laying out this book, and more importantly for your editing, input, advice, and overall expertise. I can't see how this project would have come to fruition without you.

To my husband, Ted - thank you for always supporting my work. Without you and your love, I could not have preserved countless memories for us and for others in fabric art.

To my daughters, Laura and Robin – From the first moments I held you, I wished for you mostly good memories. I pray that wish stays with you always.

To all grandparents, do not think lightly of the gifts you share with your grandchildren. Every moment is a memory etched in their hearts.

To my mom, thank you for being a mother and a father to me and for helping me to not only live, but to thrive.

And to my dad, thank you for Mémé's sewing tin. It's still with me, as are my memories of you.

Dedication and Acknowledgments from the Illustrator

To my Mom, Lola, Nana, and Mama LeDuc, and to all the people who have helped me become the woman and artist I am today. And in loving memory of Marianne Meltser, whose kindness, crafts, and memory lives on.

Mémé's Memory Quilt

Written by
Dorothy J. Szypulski

Illustrated by
Rachel L. Y. LeDuc

Mémé's Memory Quilt by Dorothy J. Szypulski
Copyright © 2022 by Dorothy J. Szypulski
ISBN: 978-1-59755-657-6
All Rights Reserved.

Illustrated by: Rachel L. Y. LeDuc

Published by: ADVANTAGE BOOKS™, www.advbookstore.com

This book and parts thereof may not be reproduced in any form, stored in a retrieval system, or transmitted in any form by any means (electronic, mechanical, photocopy, recording or otherwise) without prior written permission of the author, except as provided by United States of America copyright law.

Library of Congress Catalog Number: 2022932218

Szypulski, Dorothy, Author
LeDuc. Rachel L. Y., Illustrator
Mémé's Memory Quilt / Dorothy Szypulski , Advantage Books, 2022
ISBN (print): 9781597556576
Books > Crafts, Hobbies & Home > Needlecrafts & Textile Crafts > Quilts & Quilting
Books > Crafts, Hobbies & Home > Needlecrafts & Textile Crafts > Patchwork
Books > Crafts, Hobbies & Home > Needlecrafts & Textile Crafts > Needlework
Books > Crafts, Hobbies & Home > Home Improvement & Design > How-to & Home Improvements > Do-It-Yourself

First Printing: March 2022
22 23 24 25 26 27 10 9 8 7 6 5 4 3 2 1

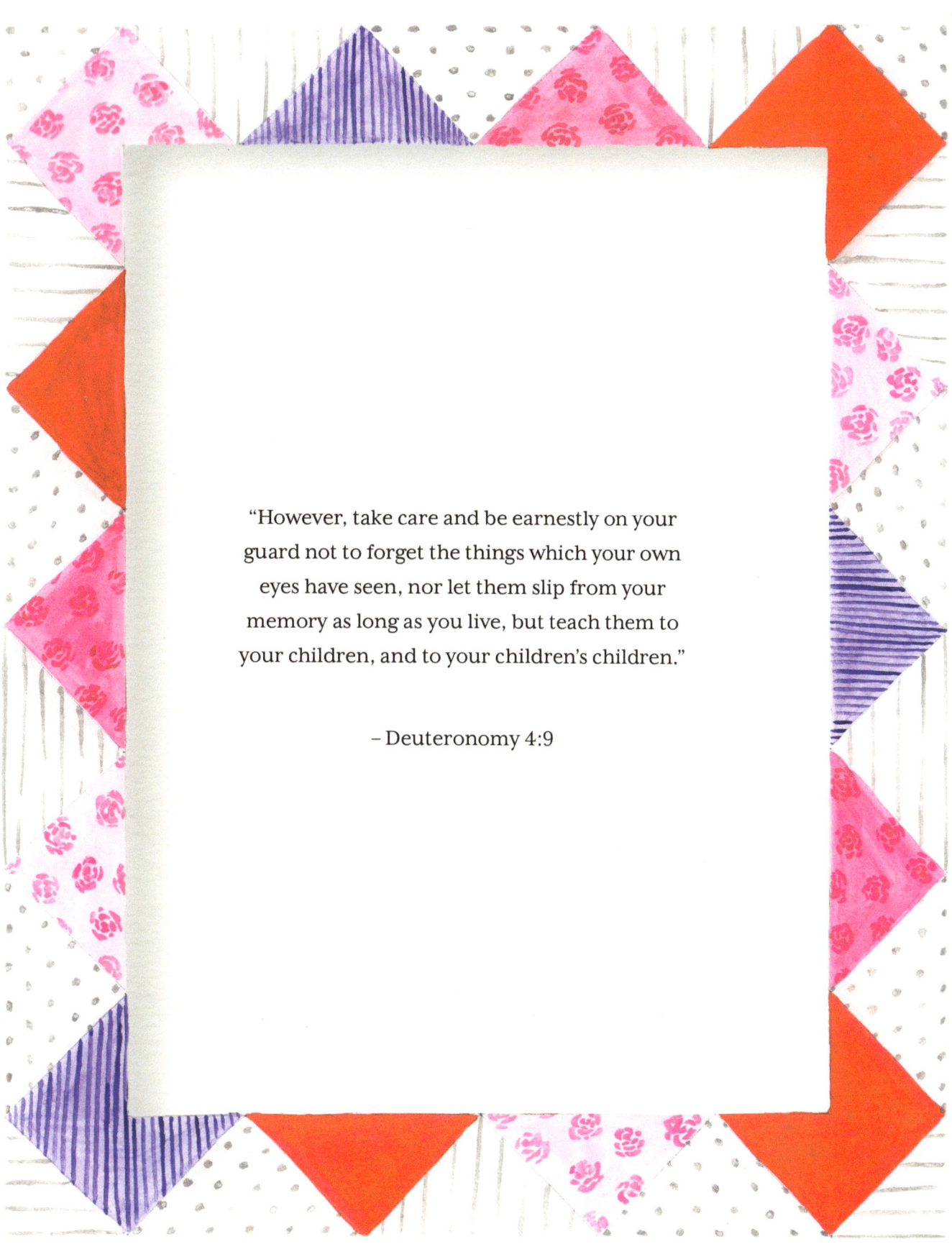

"However, take care and be earnestly on your guard not to forget the things which your own eyes have seen, nor let them slip from your memory as long as you live, but teach them to your children, and to your children's children."

– Deuteronomy 4:9

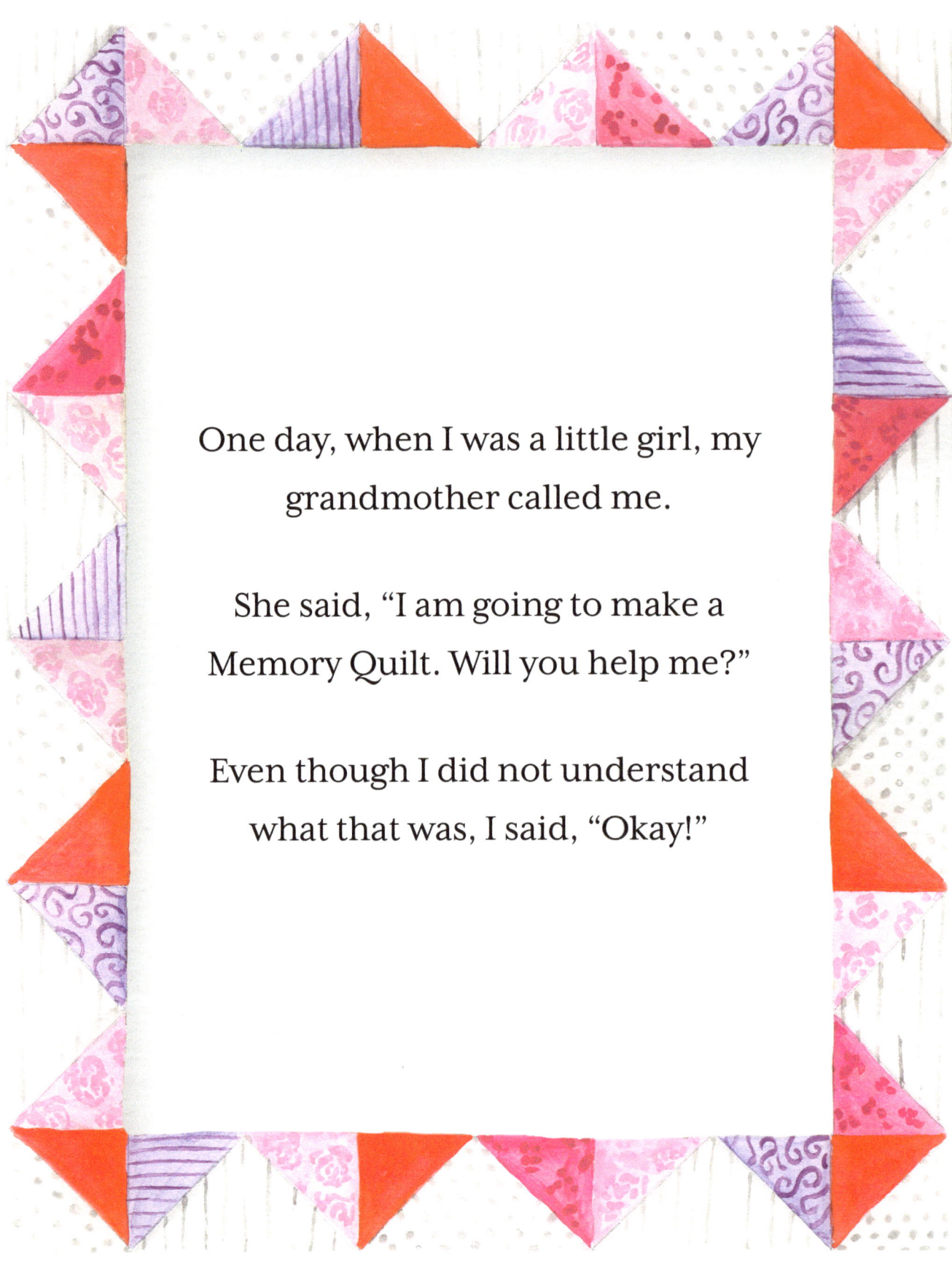

One day, when I was a little girl, my grandmother called me.

She said, "I am going to make a Memory Quilt. Will you help me?"

Even though I did not understand what that was, I said, "Okay!"

My mother drove me to Mémé
and Pépé's big yellow house
in the country.

My grandparents' home was surrounded by woods. I loved sitting by the window to watch for forest animals who came into the yard to visit.

First Mémé gave me
milk and cookies.

Then she said, "We are going to
turn our memories into a beautiful
flower garden quilt. It's going to
take a long time."

I did not understand,
but I said, "Okay."

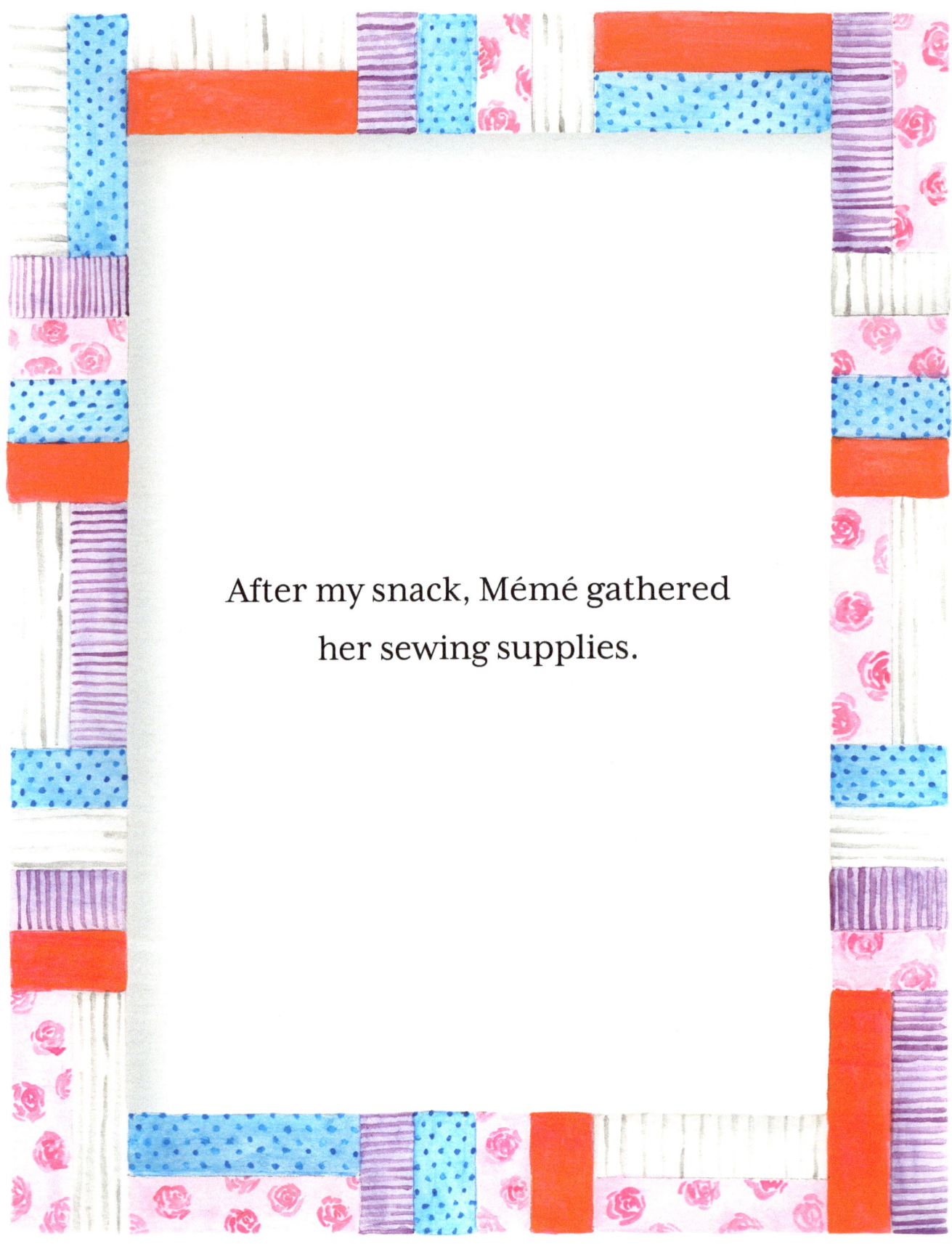

After my snack, Mémé gathered her sewing supplies.

Next, we chose fabrics stored in the sewing room.

Mémé said, "Let's pick some pretty flower colors."

"One of my favorite times was when you were born," Mémé said.

I did not understand,
but I said, "Okay."

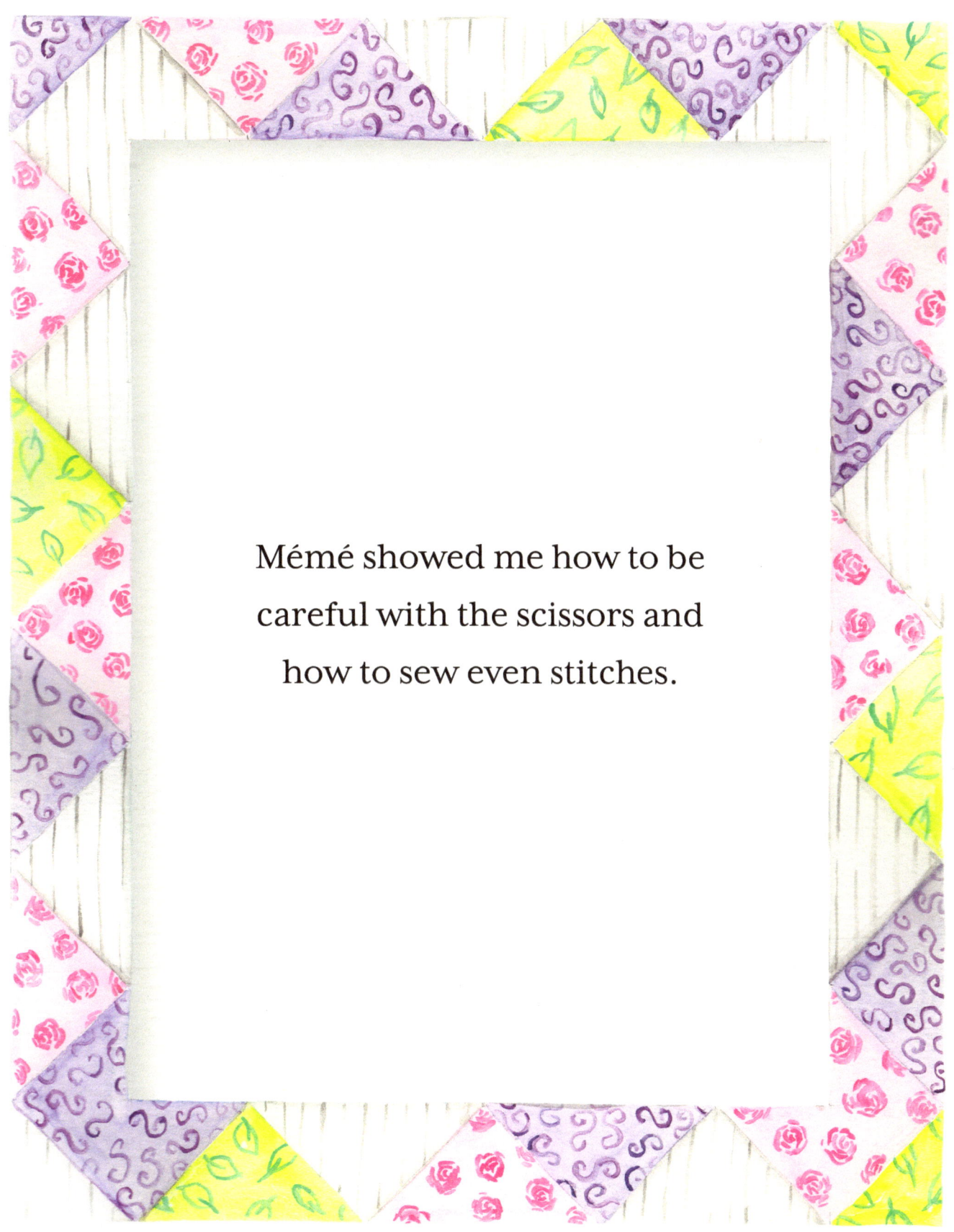

Mémé showed me how to be careful with the scissors and how to sew even stitches.

Before long, I was old enough to go to school. Many times, Mémé and I would sew after I finished my homework.

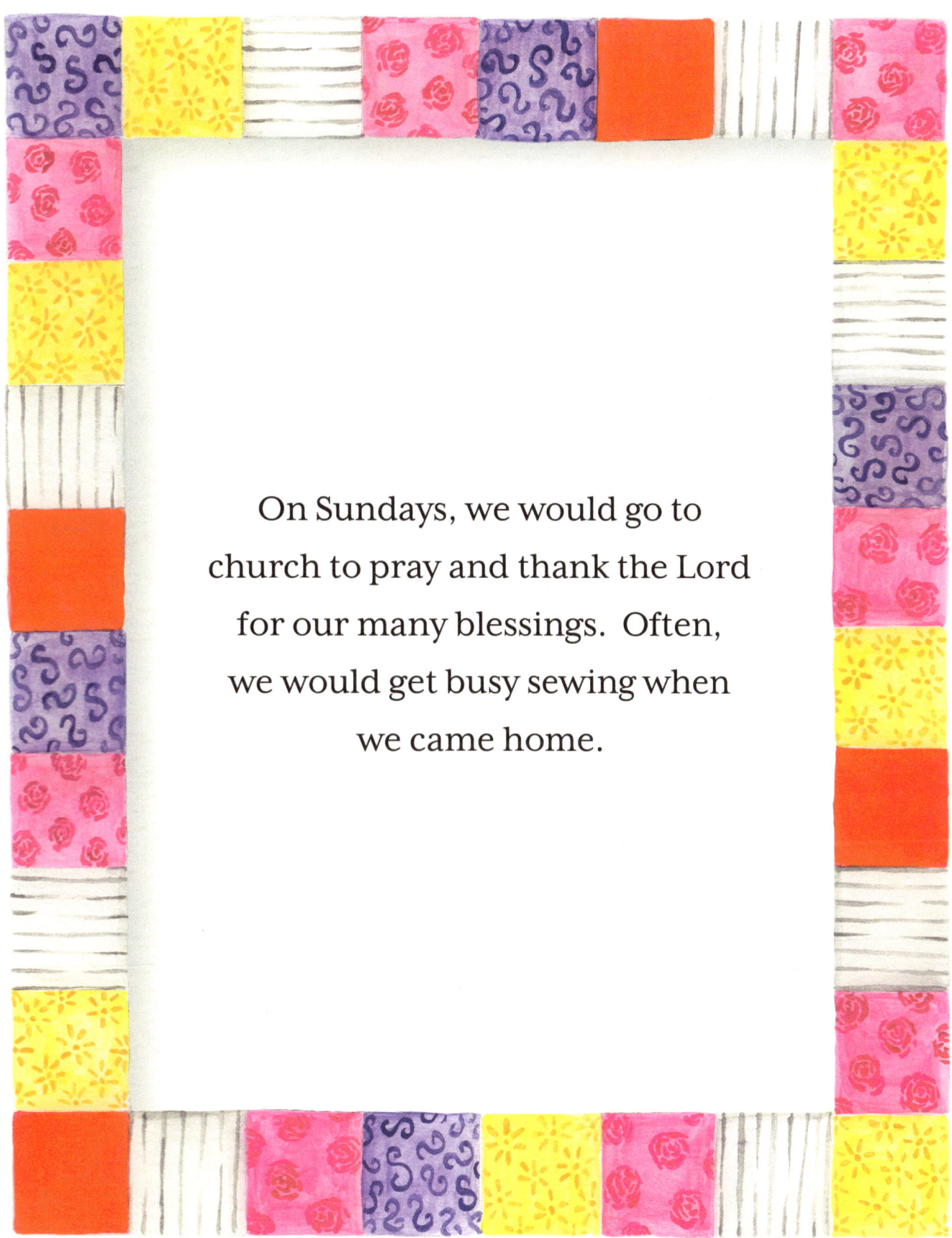

On Sundays, we would go to church to pray and thank the Lord for our many blessings. Often, we would get busy sewing when we came home.

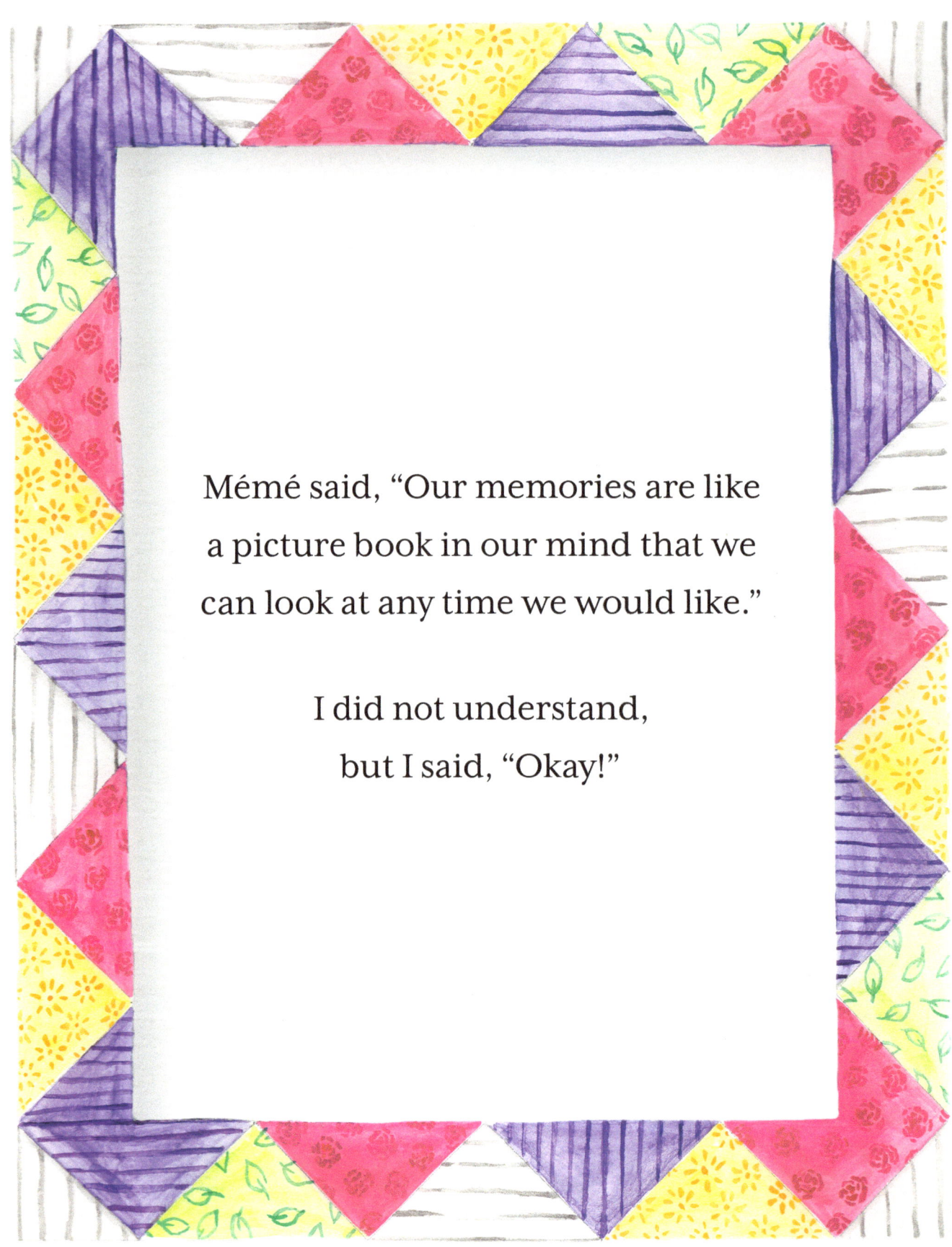

Mémé said, "Our memories are like a picture book in our mind that we can look at any time we would like."

I did not understand,
but I said, "Okay!"

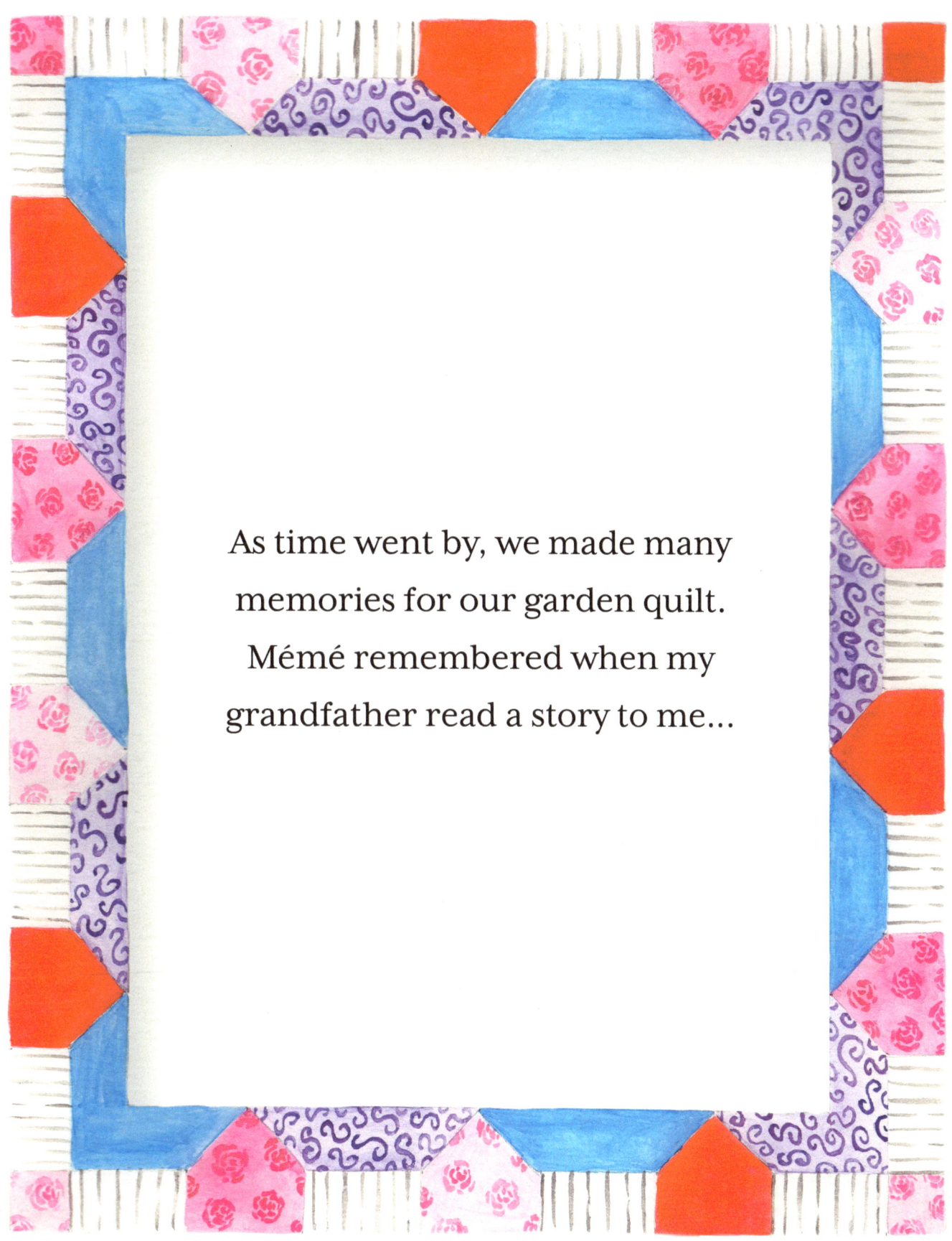

As time went by, we made many memories for our garden quilt. Mémé remembered when my grandfather read a story to me…

. . . and when he took me for a ride in his old car.

My grandmother even remembered our fun visits to amusement parks. I remember how we both loved the ferris wheel best!

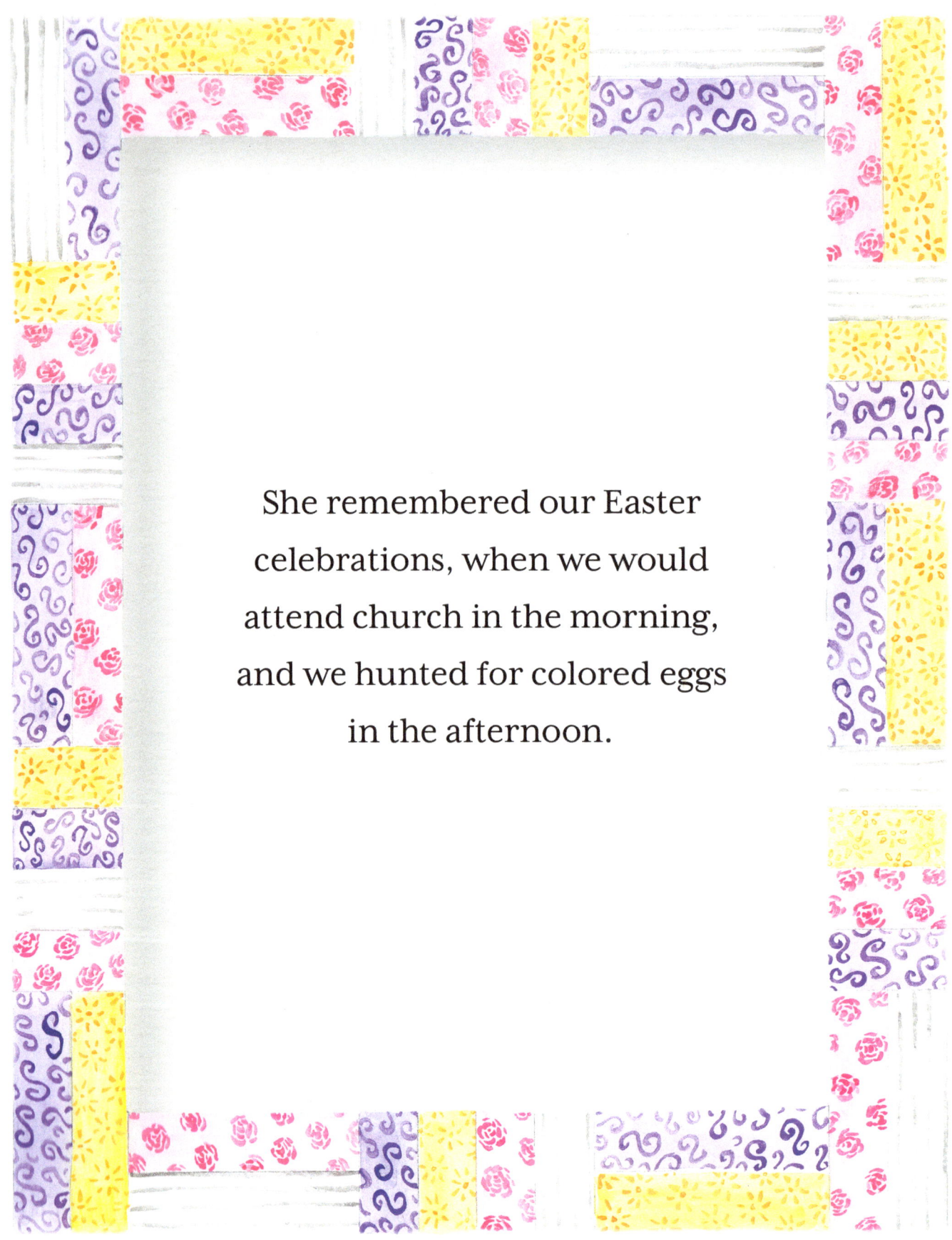

She remembered our Easter celebrations, when we would attend church in the morning, and we hunted for colored eggs in the afternoon.

Mémé remembered our family gatherings every Thanksgiving, and how I was a big help in the kitchen cooking dinner.

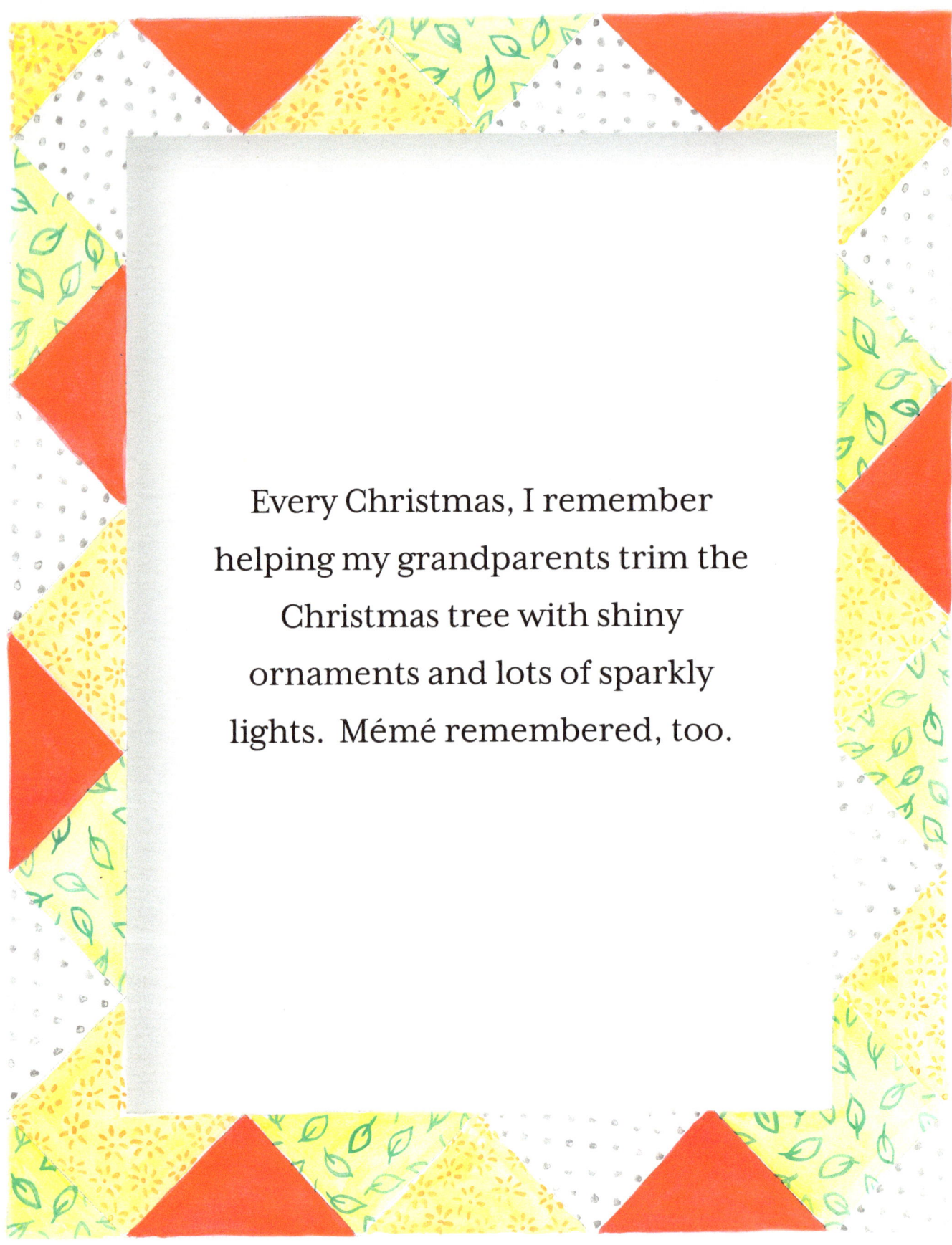

Every Christmas, I remember helping my grandparents trim the Christmas tree with shiny ornaments and lots of sparkly lights. Mémé remembered, too.

Mémé remembered all the
special occasions like anniversaries
and my birthdays.

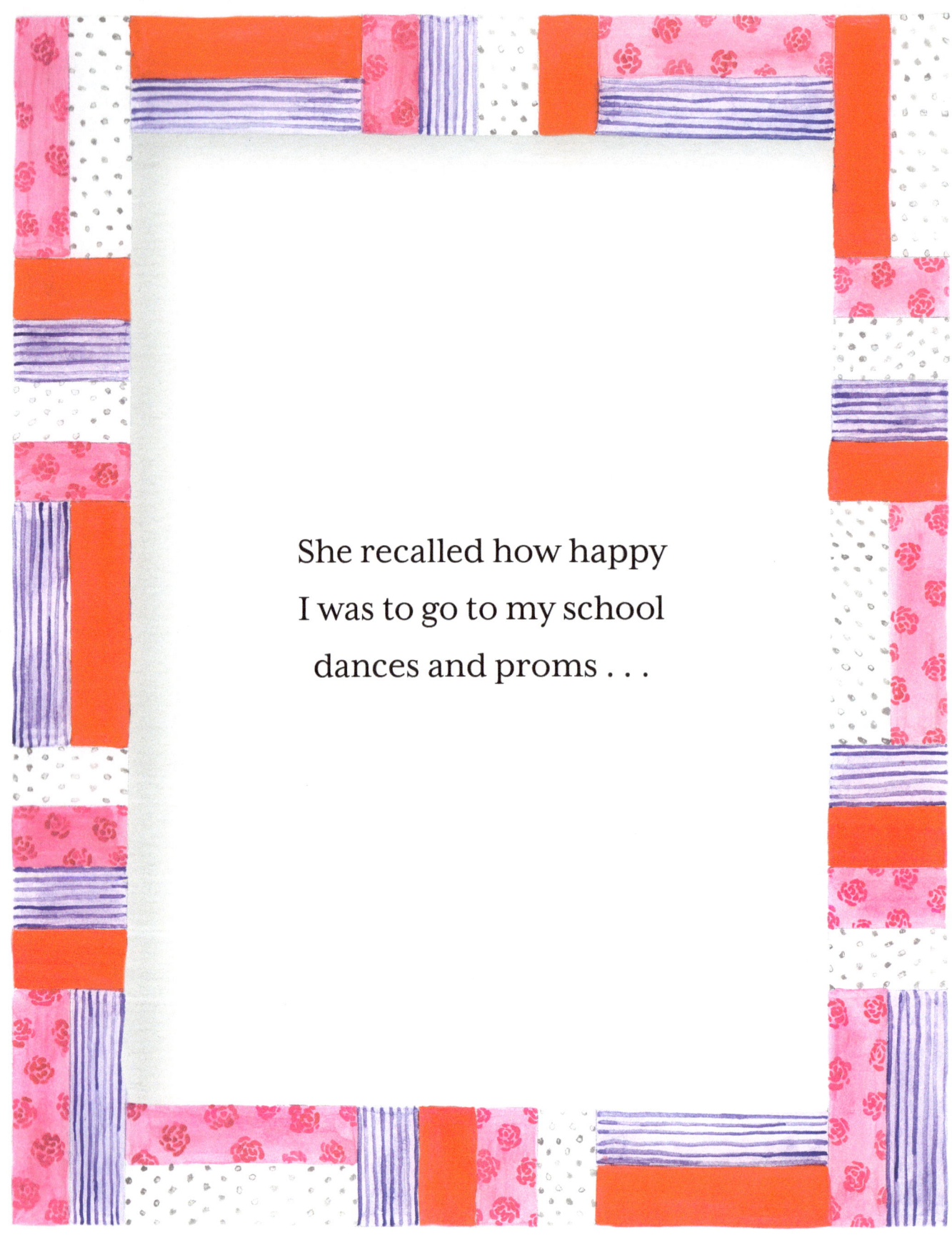

She recalled how happy
I was to go to my school
dances and proms . . .

. . . and how proud she and Pépé were when I graduated from high school and college.

Mémé and I especially enjoyed our "tea time" when we would enjoy long chats, sharing happy memories and talking about my future plans.

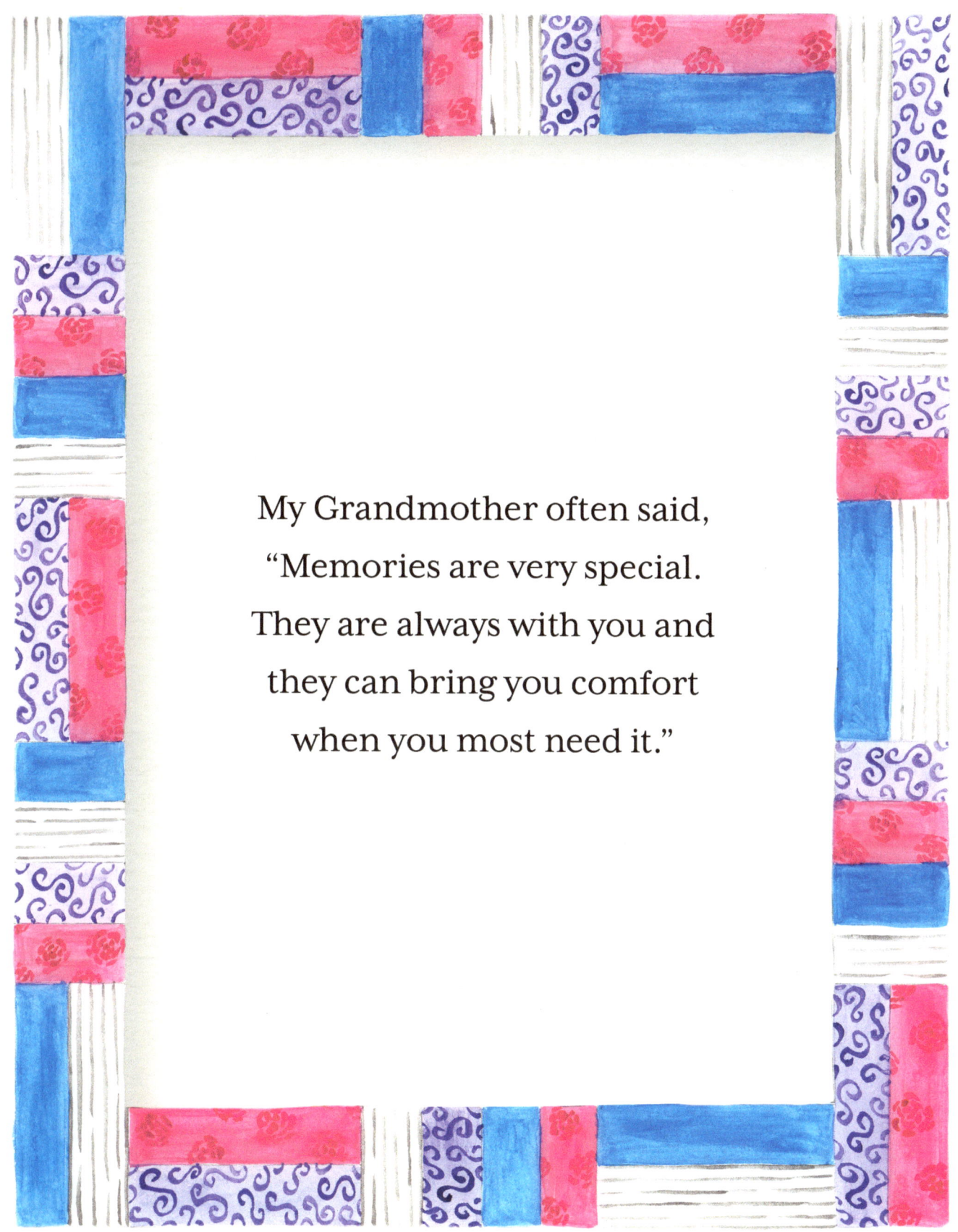

My Grandmother often said, "Memories are very special. They are always with you and they can bring you comfort when you most need it."

"Now I understand."

For more information, contact Dorothy Szypulski at: sewwrite724@gmail.com

To purchase additional copies of this book or other books published by Advantage Books visit our online bookstore at www.advbookstore.com

Longwood, Florida, USA
"we bring dreams to life"™
www.advbooks.com

www.ingramcontent.com/pod-product-compliance
Lightning Source LLC
Chambersburg PA
CBHW040056160426
43192CB00002B/82